CONCISE COLLECTION

Freshwater Fish

Trevor Housby

Grange
BOOKS

Published in 1995
by Grange Books
An imprint of Grange Books Plc.
The Grange
Grange Yard
London SE1 3AG

ISBN 1 85627 797 6

Printed in Italy.

Acknowledgments
Ardea: D. Avon 10; I. R. Beames 22, 41; P. Morris 9,
14, 16, 19, 20, 29, 30, 31, 38, 40, 45, 46.
Bruce Coleman: Hans Reinhard 7, 15, 17, 23; Michel
Roggo 32, 33.
Oxford Scientific Films: Frederick Ehrenstrom 12;
Breck P. Kent 8, 26; Zig Leszczynski 28; Colin
Milkins 4, 13, 27, 39; Avril Ramage 25.
Planet Earth Pictures: Kenneth Lucas 11, 21, 34, 42,
43, Title Page; Gilbert van Ryckevorsel 35.

All artwork by David Webb/Linden Artists.

Right: A pike with a frog in its jaws.

Contents

Introduction

To see a wild salmon jump clear of a river is one of the great sights of the natural world. The freshwater fish of Europe and America while often sharing their ancestry, exhibit a fascinating diversity of size, appearance and behavioural characteristics – such as that of the leaping salmon – that can make fish-watching an absorbing and rewarding pastime.

Not all the species of freshwater fish described in this book spend the full span of their lives in rivers and lakes. Some, such as the salmon, sea trout, shad, some sturgeon and char, spend much of their lives in saltwater, re-entering the river system of their birth to spawn, and in some cases to die. In the case of the American/European eel this process is reversed. Eels spawn then die in the weedy depths of the Sargasso Sea and the resulting young then drift on the ocean currents until they reach a river estuary.

Freshwater fish are not necessarily as small as many people assume. In the U.S.A. they can range in size from the diminutive shiners, to the huge catfish and truly enormous sturgeon. In European waters the giant Wels catfish and the sturgeon are the largest species, while minnows, sticklebacks and loach are the midgets of the streams and ponds.

All fish, irrespective of size, however, display aspects of lifestyle and behaviour that can make the study of them fascinating. The tranquil surface of a lake and the smooth flow of a river in no way reflect the turbulent life that lies beneath. Under the surface lies a world of murder and mayhem and where cannibalism is rife. Even the tiniest of fish will eat fish eggs and newly-hatched fry. At the top of this predatory chain are the catfish and the ever-voracious members of the pike family, vying with each other for the crown. These fish eat almost anything that swims or paddles on the water's surface, as well as the fish beneath it. They will eat frogs, rats and even young waterbirds. When live food is scarce they will turn scavenger, taking dead fish and animals. It is possible in an artificial environment, by selective breeding as well as removing the usual elements of competition present in the wild, to breed superior fish.

In the wild this is only achieved by a combination of luck and superior cunning. Obviously many species reach a maximum length measured in inches. Such fish usually breed more prolifically than larger fish because in turn they die in their millions to satisfy the constant hunger of the larger, major predators. Most of this day-to-day struggle for life goes undetected by man.

Fish watching is not an easy occupation or pastime. If you are familiar with your local stretch of water (and lucky enough to have one conveniently located), then fish watching is possible if you have patience and a little knowhow. You will then be rewarded with an insight into the secret lives of fish.

Fish do not always lurk only in the depths. Hot days, for example, may bring fish to bask among surface weeds and they can then be observed over long periods. Spawning time is another excellent time to watch fish, for during the spawning frenzy, normally secretive fish throw caution to the wind. At such a time thousands of large individual fish will move to a pre-selected spawning area. Such areas are normally used year after year and the spawning fish will ignore human presence in their desire to mate and shed their eggs.

Salmon are probably one of the easiest fish to watch. During their upstream run these scaly warriors perform remarkable leaps to ascend weirs and rapids, making attempt after attempt until they succeed.

Hopefully this book will show you that all fish are individuals in their own right, with their own habits and characteristics. Some are shy skulkers, others are the kings, princes and pirates of the rivers and lakes. All are fascinating.

Barbel

Classification: *Barbus barbus*, family Cyprinidae
Habitat: Fast-flowing rivers with deep pools
Range: Throughout Europe and the U.K. A smaller sub-species occurs in the Iberian Peninsular
Coloration: Greeny/bronze or black, yellow bronze on its sides with a white belly. The scales are small and neat
Size: Up to 6 kg (13.2 lb)

Description: The barbel is a large European member of the carp family. It is a long, strong-looking fish with a broad tail and large fins. The body is almost heart-shaped in cross-section the belly being flattened. As its body shape indicates it is very much a bottom-living species, living for the most part in the faster sections of large rivers. Barbel feed on small fish, worms, crustaceans (fresh-water crayfish) elvers, lampreys, insects and molluscs. The mouth of the barbel has four large, long barbules and a down-turned gape. The fish uses its mouth like a siphon, the barbules being used to feel for food in the mud and silt. Barbel have strong pharyngeal teeth (throat teeth) which are used to crush mussels, snail shells and crayfish. Barbel breed in the early spring, the eggs being shed in the weeds that grow in gravelly shallows. The yellowy, translucent eggs hatch in 12–14 days. The fry hide in the stones and weed, feeding initially on tiny insects and algae.

Large and Small Mouth Bass

Classification: Large mouth bass – *Microp-pterus salmoides*; small mouth bass – *Microp-terus dolomieue*. Family Centrarchidae

Habitat: Large mouth bass like to live among aquatic vegetation, small mouth bass prefer more open water

Range: Throughout the U.S.A.

Coloration: The large mouth bass has a green back with yellow–green sides over-layed with dark blotches. The gill covers have 3–4 horizontal dark lines. The small mouth bass has a bronze back and body with dark vertical stripes

Size: Large mouth bass reach a weight of 5–6 kg (11–13.2 lb). Small mouth bass are somewhat larger on average

Description: Bass are rough, tough, acrobatic fish associated with wild lakes, the swamps of Florida and clear, rocky rivers. Highly adaptable, the large and small mouth bass thrive in a variety of waters. Apart from the two species there are at least 6 sub-species. All the bass are thickset fish with large fins and tail. The single dorsal fin has a distinctive spiky front section, the rear portion being soft. Bass breed in late spring or early summer, the eggs being deposited on weed or submerged roots or lily stalks. Once hatched, the young fish are often attacked and eaten by their parents. Bass fry feed on zooplankton and insect larvae. Later as they develop they become true predators taking fish, tadpoles, crustaceans such as crayfish, water dogs and even small waterfowl, swimming rodent's and small snakes. Ever-watchful for surface movement, bass can often be seen taking food from the top layers of water. Left, is a large mouth bass.

Bowfin

Classification: *Amia calva,* family Amidae
Habitat: Shallow lakes and slow moving rivers
Range: Eastern and southern states of the U.S.A.
Coloration: In overall coloration the bowfin is a drab mottled brown. It has a noticeable dark spot on the base of the tail. In the male this is ringed in orange/yellow
Size: Up to 8 kg (17.6 lb) in weight

Description: The bowfin is the last remaining member of a once prolific family whose fossil remains have been unearthed in Europe and North America. A voracious predator, the bowfin shows a liking for quiet water. They eat frogs, crayfish as well as dead fish. Immature specimens also feed on aquatic insects. Long and thickset with a squat head and large mouth filled with sharp teeth, the bowfin looks every inch a predator. Its long dorsal fin and large tail obviously give it hunting speed. Internally it has a unique swim bladder that acts as a lung. This allows them to live and thrive in water with a low oxygen level. Bowfin breed in late spring. The eggs are laid in a nest constructed by the male fish. Often two or more females will share the same nest site. The eggs hatch in 8 to 10 days. During the incubation period and for a time after hatching the male aggressively stands guard. Once hatched the young fish spend a further 9 or 10 days in the weed adjacent to the nest.

Bronze Bream

Classification: *Abramis brama*, family Cyprinidae
Habitat: Still waters, slow moving rivers
Range: North Europe, England and Northern and Southern Ireland
Coloration: Body colour varies according to environment. Most common colour is deep bronze on the back, lighter bronze on the sides. The underparts are creamy white. Small bream are more silvery
Size: Bream reach a weight of 6–7 kg (13.2–15.4 lb)

Description: The bronze bream has the deepest and most laterally compressed body of all British and European freshwater species. Like the tench they produce a thick body mucus which acts as a protection for the small, neat body scales. Essentially a shoaling species, bream tend to travel and feed in large packs. Normally fish of the same year class live in such groups. As time passes natural predation causes the shoal size to decrease until it consists of only six or seven huge fish. Such fish are in the final years of their natural life span. Bream spawn in late spring, the eggs being shed in shallow, weed-infested water. Once hatched, bream fry hide and feed in the weed until they grow large enough to venture out into deeper water. Essentially a bottom-feeding species, bream feed on worms, bloodworms (midge larvae) and various nymphs and caddis larvae. Bream shoals often give away their position by rolling playfully as a prelude to a feeding spree.

Bullheads

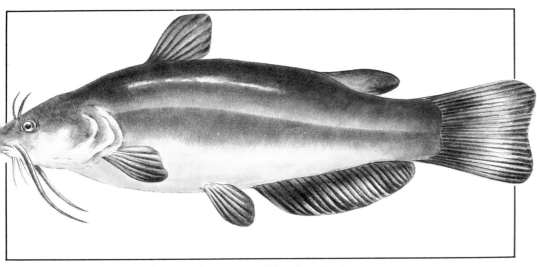

Classification: The brown bull head – *Ictalurus nebulosus*; the black bullhead – *Ictalurus melas*; the yellow bullhead – *Ictalurus natalis*; the flat bullhead – *Ictalurus platycephalus*. Family Ictaluridae

Habitat: Muddy, weedy lakes and slow moving streams

Range: N. America, parts of Mexico

Coloration: The brown bullhead is a sleek mottled brown colour. The black bullhead is green to black on the back with paler sides and a white belly. The yellow bullhead is mottled yellow. The flat bullhead is similar to the yellow but has a dark patch on the lower section of its dorsal fin

Size: 1–1.5 kg (2.2–3.3 lb)

Description: Very much classed as a pan fish, the diminutive bullhead tribe are a group of small catfish. Bullheads are similar in shape to other catfish but have a stockier, rather bulky profile. In recent years their natural range has been extended due to intensive restocking policies. One bullhead species, the black bullhead which was originally found from North Dakota south to Texas and then North east to New York has now become widespread. This same fish was introduced to France where it multiplied to plague proportions in just a few years. Fortunately bullheads make excellent eating and are much sought after by anglers. This has helped to keep their numbers in check. Bullheads spawn in late spring, seeking out shallow streams and weedy marginal shallows in which to deposit their eggs. Once hatched the young fish stay under cover, feeding for the most part on zooplankton and minute insects. Later they become scavengers feeding off live and dead fish, or animal flesh. Small bullheads are often eaten by larger, predatory fish. Right, is a yellow bullhead.

Burbot

Classification: *Lota lota*, family Gadidae
Habitat: Rivers and stream–fed lakes
Range: North America, Europe and Asia
Coloration: Dark olive above with chainlike blackish or yellowish markings on the side
Size: Normally 0.5 kg (1.1 lb)

Description: Burbot are a freshwater member of the cod family. The body is elongated and rather eel-like. The head is rather flat, and has a short barbel on each nostril. A single, longer barbel projects from the burbot's chin. The back of the fish carries two dorsal fins. The first fin is short, the second very long. The anal fin is similar in length and shape to the second dorsal fin. The scales are deeply embedded in the tough skin. Very much a deep water fish burbot, have been taken in depths of up to 213 m (700 ft). In the U.S.A. burbot are found from New England, the Susquehanna River system in the east, and throughout the Hudson Bay drainage area, as well as the Columbia river. In Britain the fish are now very rare and only occur in East Anglia. Burbot spawn in February, usually under ice, the eggs being shed at night. Burbot are also nocturnal feeders, eating crayfish and any live or dead fish which comes their way.

Carp

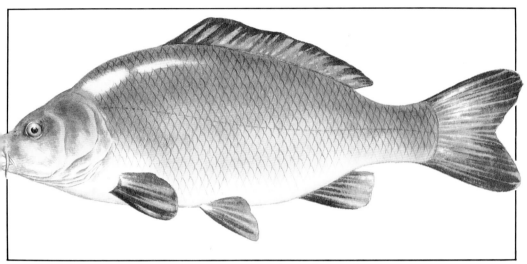

Classification: *Cyprinus carpio*, family Cyprinidae

Habitat: Normally a pond or lake fish, carp can, and will, adapt to life in large rivers

Range: Practically world-wide

Coloration: Carp vary considerable in colour, the normal colour being olive bronze with yellow- or chestnut-coloured flanks. The belly is paler

Size: Carp can reach weights in excess of 40 kg (88 lb). The normal run of fish is 1.8–3.6 kg (4–8 lb)

Description: Originating in Asia, carp were farmed as early as 400 B.C. Over the centuries its range increased, often by deliberate introduction. The first such stocking in Britain took place in the mid–15th century. In the United States carp were not stocked until 1876, the first fish being brought from Germany and placed in ponds near Baltimore. They became widely distributed throughout North America, but it was soon realized that carp were doing great damage to the natural balance of American waters. Now the fish are regarded as little more than vermin. Originally, all carp were long-bodied, fully-scaled fish. These early fish, known as wild carp, are slow growing. Selective breeding by European fish farmers produced a new strain of fish which grew rapidly. These fish, known as king carp, can be fully scaled or have just a few large scales. Carp feeds on shrimps, worms, molluscles, larvae and nymphs. The mouth of the carp has four barbules used as an aid to feeding. They breed in late spring and early summer, one female often being attended by a number of smaller males.

Catfish (U.S.A.)

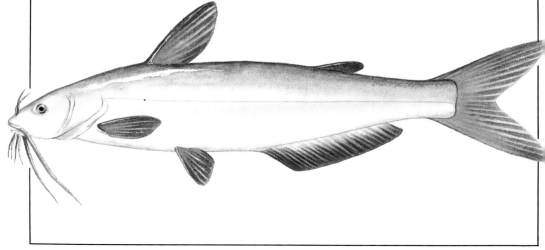

Classification: Blue catfish – *Ictalurus furcatus*; channel catfish – *Ictalurus punctatus*; white catfish – *Ictalurus catus*; flathead catfish – *Pylodictis olivaris*. Family Ictaluridae

Habitat: Large lakes and clearwater rivers. Occasionally deep, clear streams

Range: Catfish of one sort or another are found throughout the U.S.A.

Coloration: The blue catfish has a blue back, paler flanks and silver white body. The channel catfish is similar but its body colour is overlaid with dark spots and blotches. The flathead catfish is a mottled brown colour. The white catfish is silvery white

Size: Blue catfish 25–40 kg (55–88 lb). Channel catfish 10–20 kg (22–44 lb). Flathead catfish 25–40 kg (55–88 lb). White catfish 1–1.5 kg (2.2–3.3 lb)

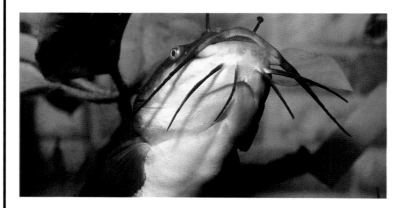

Description: An elongated, ugly family of fish, the catfish tribe have two widely-spaced dorsal fins, a long anal fin and a broad powerful tail. All American catfish have two short barbules on the top of the snout, two long barbules extending back from the corner of their jaws and four slender barbules projecting from the underside of the jaw. Several species of American catfish are prized for the quality of their firm white flesh. Many fish farms now specialize in raising both the channel catfish and the white catfish for an ever-expanding market. In the young state catfish live on insects, water snails and tiny fish. Once maturity is reached live and dead fish, or small animals make up the mainstay of their diet. The larger species also take ducklings and the young of other water birds. In deep water catfish may feed during the day, while shallow water fish show nocturnal tendencies. The eggs are shed in spring, normally around submerged weed beds. The channel catfish, however, migrates from lakes and large rivers to spawn in small sidestreams.

Catfish (Wels)

Classification: *Silurus glanis*, family Siluridae

Habitat: Catfish are found in muddy lakes, large, slow flowing rivers and some European reservoirs

Range: Throughout eastern and central Europe and in selected parts of Britain

Coloration: Normally a dark, mottled brown with yellow blotched sides and yellow white underparts. Albino catfish also occur

Size: In Britain Wels attain a weight of around 20 kg (44 lb). In Europe fish up to 100 kg (220 lb) occur. The largest recorded fish weighed 280 kg (617 lb) and came from the River Dneiper in the U.S.S.R.

Description: The Wels or Danubian catfish is the largest of the world's fifteen catfish families. In the wild it can reach a length of over $4\frac{1}{4}$ m (14.7 ft). The Wels is an ugly fish with a long, tapering body and tiny, stunted tail. Its head is huge and flattened. The mouth is large with strong rubbery lips and many small teeth. From the hinge of the upper jaw two very long barbules project. Four smaller barbules hang below the fish's chin. Wels were introduced into Britain approximately 100 years ago, the first fish being stocked into Woburn Abbey lakes by the then Duke of Bedford. Since the original stocking catfish have been introduced into other localities. Wels spawn in early spring, and the eggs are shed in marginal weed beds. Despite its ungainly shape the Wels is an active hunter. Much of its food consists of fish, but it will also take frogs, rats, small waterbirds and dead creatures. Mainly a nocturnal species, this giant catfish spends most of the daylight hours in the shelter of dense weedbeds. Occasionally during hot, thundery weather it will indulge in a daylight feeding frenzy.

Char

Classification: *Salvelinus alpinus,* family Salmonidae

Habitat: In its migratory form this fish is found in Alaska, Greenland, Canada, Iceland and northern Norway. Landlocked char occur in Great Britain, Ireland, Germany, Scandinavia and the U.S.S.R.

Coloration: Migratory char are greenish silver with light blotches. Landlocked char are greeny brown with an orange red belly and yellow white spots

Size: Char normally weigh from 0.5–1.5 kg (1.1–3.3 lb)

Description: Although quite a primitive species char, or arctic char, are very beautiful, highly edible little fish. The landlocked variety became so as a result of the last Ice Age. In Britain these can be found in lakes Windermere and Coniston. Some Scottish lochs also hold char, although stocks are thought to be rapidly diminishing. On Windermere, char were once caught commercially on spinner baits hammered out of gold sovereigns. Migratory char spend most of their year at sea, returning in the late summer to spawn in the rivers of their birth. Non-migratory char spawn in late winter or early spring, making a short migration from the very deep, central lake sections to the comparatively shallow marginal banks. A close relative is the Dolly Varden or bull trout, *Salvelinus malma,* which is found in the lakes and rivers of the northern Pacific basin. The range of this species extends from north California to Japan and Korea.

Chub

Classification: *Leuciscus cepaalus*, family Cyprinidae

Habitat: Chub are normally found in rivers and streams. They have also been stocked in lakes where they seem to thrive

Coloration: The back is bronze or slate grey giving way to silver gold sides and white underparts. The pelvic and anal fins are orange red, the dorsal and tail fins, blue grey

Size: Chub commonly reach a weight of 2–2.5 kg (4.4–5.5 lb)

Description: Thick-bodied with a large head and huge toothless mouth the chub is a wary fish. Much of its life is spent skulking among the roots of trees at the water's edge or between thick weed beds and it rarely ventures out into open water. Chub are omniverous but prefer to feed on small fish, crayfish and caddis larvae. They also wait under overhanging trees where they intercept fallen insects and berries. It is found in most English river systems, selected Scottish rivers and many parts of Europe. Spawning occurs in late spring, the fish gathering on fast gravelly shallows to shed their eggs on streamer weed and the roots of bankside trees. Like most fish, chub are to a degree cannibalistic, eating young fish of their own kind. Despite having toothless jaws, chub have extremely strong throat teeth (pharyngeal teeth). These are used to crush and grind up tough items. Izaak Walton, whose book *The Compleat Angler* was published in 1853, called the chub by its old English name of Chavander.

Black and White Crappies

Classification: Black crappie – *Pomoxis nigromaculatus*; white crappie – *Pomoxis annularis*. Family Centrarchidae
Habitat: Ponds, lakes, rivers and in the case of the black crappie brackish water
Range: Widely distributed through the U.S.A.
Coloration: The black crappie has a blue–grey back and silvery sides. The sides are overlaid with dark markings that collectively form horizontal bands. The white crappie is lighter coloured with dark vertical bars
Size: The black crappie reaches a weight of 1.5 kg (3.3 lb), the white crappie is larger reaching 2–2.5 kg (4.4–5.5 lb)

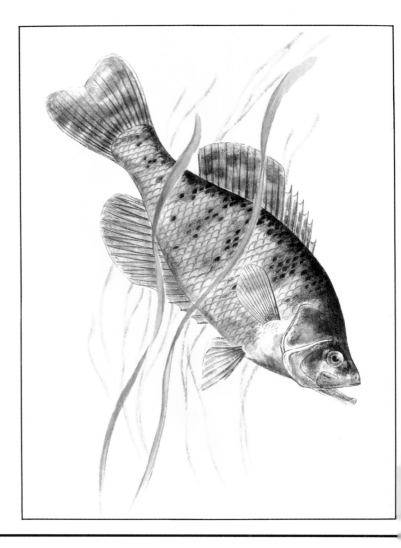

Description: The crappies are extremely popular pan fish. They are deep-bodied, handsome fish with large, well-formed and armed fins. The anal fin of the black crappie has six strong spines and the dorsal fin 7–8 spines. The white crappie has only 6 dorsal fin spines. Very much a skulking species, the crappie prefers to live and feed in deep water, or preferably amongst tree stumps, brush piles and other underwater obstructions. Both species breed in late spring, the eggs being deposited amongst various water weeds. The black crappie is very much a clear water species. The white crappie on the other hand will tolerate murky, rather turgid water. Very much opportunist feeders, both crappie varieties will feed on whatever happens to be readily available. Shrimps, nymphs, small fish, water beetles, are all taken in season. Seldom found close to the surface, crappie are mainly a mid-water species, taking much of their food from reed stems and other upwardly projecting objects. Due to over exploitation by sportsmen large crappie are now something of a rarity.

Dace

Classification: *Leuciscus leuciscus*, family Cyprinidae

Habitat: Very much a river and stream fish, the dace prefers shallow well-oxygenated water

Coloration: The back of the dace is olive grey. The sides bright, burnished silver. The underparts white. The dorsal and tail fins are grey. The anal and pectoral fins are tinged with a warm pink

Size: Dace reach a maximum weight of 0.5 kg (1.1 lb)

Description: The dace is a slim fish, almost round in the cross section. Its head and mouth are small and neat in appearance. Small chub are often confused with large dace. Identifying one from the other is, however, simple, for dace have a concave anal fin while chub have a convex anal fin. Dace are common in England and Wales but rare in Scotland. In Ireland they are found in only a few rivers. As a species dace are widespread in Europe and in Asia. They feed mainly on aquatic insects which they take either as nymphs or in the free flying version. Normally a shoal species, dace often congregate by the thousand. Like trout, dace often give away their position by rising freely to floating insects. Dace normally spawn in late spring, choosing the shallow water at the tail end of deep pools to shed their eggs. Once hatched, the fry hide amongst the larger stones feeding on microscopic water animals. Later as they grow larger they move to deeper water and rejoin the parent shoal.

Eel

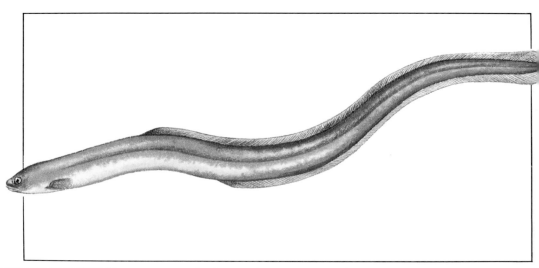

Classification: The European eel *Anguilla anguilla* and the American Eel *Anguilla rostrata* are closely related species. Family Anguillidae

Habitat: The eel is found in ponds, rivers, lakes, reservoirs and even water-filled ditches

Coloration: Normally a yellow brown colour, eels change to silver as they approach sexual maturity

Size: Most eels weigh 1–2 kg (2.2–4.4 lb). Individuals can reach a weight of over 4 kg (8.8 lb)

Description: Eels spend most of their lives in freshwater. Unlike the other fish described in this book, however, they spawn in saltwater, in this case the Sargasso Sea, an area of the North Atlantic where seaweed accumulates as a result of converging ocean currents. Once they have spawned, they die. The young when hatched, start life as a transparent, leaf-shaped creature which develops into an elongated, transparent eel. These creatures drift with the ocean currents until they reach a river estuary. The journey for the European eels from the Sargasso to Europe takes about three years. The journey for the American eel lasts only about a year. By the time they arrive in European waters they have become elvers, tiny replicas of their parents. Large numbers of these are commercially netted as they run up major river estuaries. Those that evade the nets travel by night, some even leaving the water to travel overland to lakes unconnected to the river system. Female eels are larger than the males. Later in life the urge to breed sends them back to the Sargasso.

Alligator Gar

Classification: Nine species. The largest is the alligator gar, *Lepistosteus spatula*. Family Lepisosteidae

Habitat: Bayou, and river systems including river-linked lakes

Range: From north-east Mexico to the Mississippi valley, Missouri and Kentucky

Coloration: Bronze brown on the back with darker blotches on the rear portion of the body. The underparts are dirty white

Size: Alligator gar reach a length of more than 3 m and a weight of more than 125 kg (275.5 lb)

Description: Largest of the freshwater gars, the alligator gar also has the broadest snout of its kind. Somewhat like an elongated pike in shape, the dorsal and anal fins of the gar are set well back on its long, streamlined body. The mouth or beak is long and filled with large sharp teeth. The skin on the underside of the lower jaw is elasticated to enable the gar to catch and swallow large fish. Nine species of gar are found in American waters. The most important are the longnose jar (*L. osseus*) shortnose gar (*L. platostomus*) spotted jar (*L. oculatus*) and the Florida gar (*L. platyrhincus*). All are smaller than the mighty alligator gar. The longnose reaches a weight of 25 kgs (55 lb). This species is also the commonest and most widely distributed. The freshwater gars are part of an ancient family or predatory fish. Gars are unique in that they can survive in poorly-oxygenated waters. Their air bladders are supplied with blood vessels that enable the bladder to be used as a primitive lung.

Grayling

Classification: The European grayling, *Thymallus thymallus* is closely related to the American or Arctic grayling, *Thymallus arcticus*. Family Salmonidae

Habitat: Grayling live in swift-flowing, gravel-bottomed rivers and streams which are well-oxygenated

Range: European grayling are found in England, Scotland, and north Europe. American grayling from Alaska to Saskatchewan.

Coloration: The back and sides of the grayling are silver grey spotted with irregular black blotches. The huge dorsal fin is spotted and edged in red

Size: Up to 2.5 kg (5.5 lb)

Description: Extremely beautiful, the grayling are freshwater members of the salmon family, and are survivors from the Ice Age. The grayling has a long slim body and pointed snout. The jaws and gill plates are bony, the scales hard. The adipose fin is tiny but the dorsal fin is huge. The dorsal fin of the male is low in the front and rises towards the rear; that of the female is smaller and is high in the front sloping away at the rear. Grayling eat small fish, aquatic and surface insects, freshwater shrimps, nymphs and water snails. Breeding takes place in early spring when the fish move upstream to spawn on the headwater shallows of their parent river. During the past 100 years grayling have been introduced to many rivers. Extremely sensitive to pollution, grayling will not tolerate anything but the purest of waters. Prolific spawners, grayling can quickly overpopulate some suitable rivers and so are regarded as little more than vermin on trout and salmon rivers.

Huchen

Classification: *Huch hucho*, family Salmonidae
Habitat: Large rivers and lakes
Range: The Danube river system. Subspecies occur in Siberia and Japan
Coloration: Dark brown/dark violet on the back, reddish sides and silver underparts. The body surface is covered in minute dark spots
Size: Huchen reach a weight of 20–25 kg (44–55 lb)

Description: The huchen is one of four Eurasian salmonids. Similar in shape to the Atlantic Salmon, it has a larger head and adipose fin. The body scales are much smaller than those of trout and salmon. Huchen grow extremely quickly and in good years their average annual weight increase is 2 kg (4.4 lb). Huchen spawn between March and April, the adults migrating upstream into smaller tributary rivers. The eggs are deposited in clean gravel where the water is shallow and well-oxygenated. The female digs the nest, the eggs are shed, fertilized and covered up. Like all salmon young, the fry hatch bearing a large yolk sac. Once the sac is used up the young fish begin to feed on tiny crustaceans. At this stage their growth rate begins to accelerate and they turn into true predators. Initially the young fish travel and feed in shoals. Once they become totally predatory they become solitary feeders, taking up prime feeding positions in weirs and deep holes in the river bed. Many futile attempts have been made to raise huchen on commercial fish farms.

Muskellunge

MUSKELLUNGE

Classification: *Esox masquinongy* – Great Lakes muskellunge; *Esox masquinongy immaculatus* of Minnesota and Wisconsin; *Esox masquinongy ohioensis* – Chantauqua or Ohio muskellunge. Family Esocidae
Habitat: A deep lake or river fish
Range: The Great Lakes, the Eastern lakes and the Ohio drainage as far south as Georgia
Coloration: The back of the adult muskellunge is olive bronze shading to bronze on the sides. The body colour is overlaid by dark blotches
Size: Muskellunge reach weights in excess of 25 kg (55 lb)

Description: The muskellunge or muskie is very much the prince of pike. Somewhat slimmer in build than the European pike (*Esox lucius*) it is a long, streamlined fish obviously built for short bursts of high speed. Like all pike the dorsal and anal fins of the muskellunge are set well back on the body. The jaws are large and powerful and filled with long sharp teeth. The roof of the mouth has additional pads of gripping teeth. Muskellunge are opportunist feeders living for the most part on fish. They also devour swimming snakes, frogs, water birds and muskrats. A natural cannibal, these fish will attack and eat smaller muskellunge. Muskies usually skulk in weed and reed beds poised in ambush for anything edible that comes within range. Muskellunge spawn in early spring, the huge females being well attended by the smaller male fish. Once hatched the young fish start life in the weedy shallows out of reach of their ever hungry parents. Once very common, muskellunge are now decreasing, over-fishing and pollution taking a constant toll of young and mature fish.

Perch

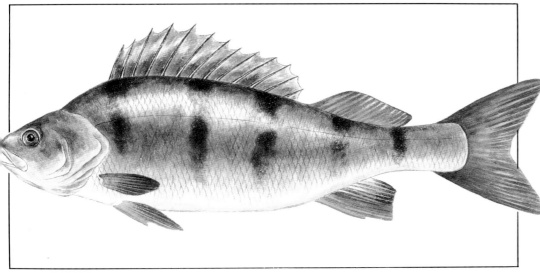

Classification: European perch – *Perca fluviatilis*; yellow perch – *Perca flavescens*. Family Pereidae

Habitat: Lakes, ponds, reservoirs and rivers

Coloration: The European perch is dark olive on the back with golden sides marked by vertical dark bars. The yellow perch is similar but of much lighter colour. The pelvic and anal fins are red

Size: Perch reach a maximum weight of around 2.5 kg (5.5 lb)

Description: The European perch is a freshwater shoal fish found throughout the British Isles and much of Europe. It also occurs in South Africa, Australasia and Asia. The closely-related yellow perch is very definitely an American and southern Canadian species. A big perch is a bold, attractive, rather chunky fish. The body is oval in cross section and as the fish begins to grow it develops a pronounced humped back. Perch have two separate dorsal fins, the first armed with long sharp spines. Only the first spine of the second dorsal is sharp. Perch scales are rough to the touch and the gill plate culminates in a sharp bony spike. Perch feed naturally on worms, small fish, nymphs and larvae, as well as many small perch. Very much a skulking species, they are often found close to beds of reed and bullrush, their striped bodies blending in with the aquatic vegetation. In recent years vast numbers of small perch have been wiped out by a recurring disease. Perch breed in late spring, the eggs being shed onto convenient soft weed beds.

Pickerels

Classification: The chain pickerel – *Esox niger*; the red fin pickerel – *Esox americanus americanus*; grass pickerel – *Esox americanus vermiculatus*. Family Esocidae

Range: The chain pickerel is common in the eastern U.S.A., the Atlantic States, Georgia and Florida. The red fin is found in the Atlantic drainage, the grass pickerel in the Mississippi and Great Lakes areas

Coloration: The chain pickerel is olive grey blotched with yellow green. The red fin pickerel is marked by vertical lines and light orange red fins

Habitat: Weedy marginal shallows

Size: Chain pickerel reach a weight of 4 kg (8.8 lb) The red fin and grass pickerel are much smaller

Description: The pickerels are all small American members of the pike family and in shape and body structure they are similar to European pike. Their jaws are lined with strong, sharp teeth. Pickerel feed on any small, live creature that comes their way. Being comparatively small they take much of their food directly from the week and lake or river bed. Caddis larvae and snails make up part of their diet, as well as small fish, including the young of their own kind. The largest of the pickerel will also take frogs, newts and small rodents. The smallest, the grass pickerel, is almost exclusively an insect eater. Owing to their small average size pickerel only thrive in waters which contain no larger pike. Pickerel spawn in early spring, the eggs being shed on weed growing in the marginal shallows. Once the fry hatch they begin to feed on zooplankton before moving on to larger food items. Highly camouflaged, pickerel are a difficult fish to see in the water, often lurking where the weed is at its thickest. Left is a red fin pickerel.

The Pike or Northern Pike

Classification: *Esox lucius*, family Esocidae

Range: Throughout Europe, Ireland, the U.S.A. and most of northern Europe and parts of North Africa

Habitat: Common in still and running water. Normally found in close proximity to weed

Coloration: Bronze or olive green on the back. Flanks light olive with an overlay of creamy spots and blotches. The fins are red to yellow, the underside white

Size: Can reach a weight of 25 kg (55 lb)

Description: Perfectly adapted for a life of murder and mayhem, the pike blends in with beds of water weed. The fins and tail are large, giving the fish rapid acceleration as and when required. The head of the pike is flattened and the large eyes are set high up in the skull. It's jaws are large, strong and bony. The teeth are long and pointed and there is a ridge of sharp but small teeth on the roof of the fish's mouth. Lazy by inclination pike, are often happy to scavenge on dead food. They are also active and effective hunters, more than capable of catching fish of up to half their own body weight. They also attack and swallow duckling and the young of many water fowl. Rats, voles, frogs are also taken freely. Pike spawn in early spring. The eggs being shed on sunken tree roots or reed stems. Once hatched the young pike quickly become predators, often catching and eating young pike of their own size. Old records indicate that pike over 50 kg (110 lb) were once caught.

Pumpkinseed

Classification: *Lepomis gibbosus*, family Centrarchidae

Range: From the Dakotas and Iowa through to the Eastern Seaboard

Habitat: Natural preference for lakes and ponds but it can be found in slow-flowing rivers

Coloration: The basic body colour is olive green. This ground colour is overlaid with attractive blue and yellow spots. Electric blue lines run from the corner of the mouth to the edge of the gill plates, each gill plate having a distinctive red tipped black spot

Size: Pumpkinseed rarely reach a weight of more than 0.25 kg (0.55 lb)

Description: Widely considered to be the prettiest of all north American panfish the pumpkinseed is a distinctive, colourful little fish. Sometimes called the common sunfish, the pumpkinseed spawns from May to early August. The eggs are laid in a crude nest scooped out of the mud or gravel. Once the eggs are shed the brightly-coloured male stands guard over the nest. Despite its diminutive size the male is aggressive enough to drive away most predators. This protective guard duty continues for several days after the fry have hatched. Once the guard fish is satisfied that the fry can look after themselves it loses interest and wonders away in search of food. The diet of the adult pumpkinseed includes snails, beetles, nymphs and occasionally any small fish including the young of its own kind. The fry feed mainly on zooplankton. Pumpkinseed are very much a fish of the weedbeds. Strong swimmers, they spend much of their life cruising between one weed bed and another in search of food.

Roach

Classification: *Rutilus rutilus*, family Cyprinidae
Habitat: Lakes, ponds, rivers, canals, and reservoirs
Range: Throughout Great Britain, Southern Ireland, Northern Ireland and Europe
Coloration: Blue/grey on the back shading to bright silvery flanks. The underside is creamy white. All fins are tinged red, the brightest being the pelvic and anal fins
Size: Up to a maximum of 2 kg

Description: Adult roach are hump-backed, deep-bodied fish. The body section is oval. Shape may change slightly depending on environment, fast river roach being slimmer than fish taken from still waters. Very much a shoaling species, roach may gather in their hundreds. Shoals often mix with rudd and bream shoals, and when spawning occurs, usually in late spring or early summer, roach fertilize the eggs of these other species and vice versa. The result is roach – rudd/roach – bream hybrids. Roach feed on snails, spawn including frog and toad, midge larvae and a wide variety of nymphs, snails and shrimps. When young fish are abundant, roach will also indulge in a little cannibalism. Normally a bottom feeder, roach will also rise to the surface to take hatching insects. On many waters roach tend to overbreed leading to a stunted fish population due to lack of natural food. Much preyed on by pike and big perch, roach only survive due to sheer numbers of fish. Prolific breeders, roach are quick to colonize new waters. In S. Ireland roach greatly extend their range during each new season.

Rudd

Classification: *Scardinius erythrophthalmus*, family Cyprinidae

Habitat: Still waters and slow-flowing rivers

Range: Common throughout England, Ireland and much of Europe

Coloration: The back is olive shading into bright gold flanks. The underside is creamy yellow. All the fins are brilliant orange/yellow. There is also a rather rare lemon-finned variant

Size: Maximum size is around 2 kg (4.4 lb)

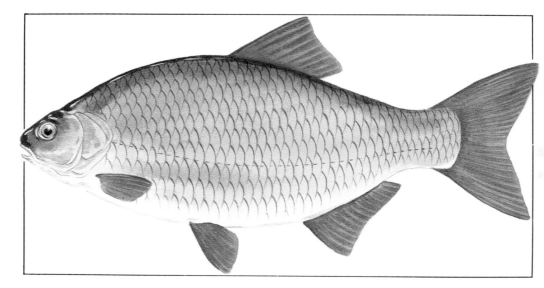

Description: Rudd are probably the most beautiful of all European shoal fish. Once called the 'golden fish of the lake', the rudd with its rather gentle nature well lives up to its name. Occasionally confused with the more silvery roach, the golden coloured rudd has a distinctive protruding lower jaw and its dorsal fin is set further back. Rudd are more inclined to surface feed than roach, much of their food being flying insects – mayfly, crane fly and various sedges. On warm evenings when fly life is abundant shoaling rudd will rise like trout. In colder weather the fish revert to bottom feeding, taking shrimps, worms, caddis larvae. On occasion the larger fish may also hunt down and catch newly-netted fish fry, including their own offspring. Spawning takes place is late spring and early summer, the eggs being shed amongst reed stems and on submerged weed beds. The lemon-finned rudd, is found in estate lakes. There is a golden rudd used as an ornamental pond fish.

Atlantic Salmon

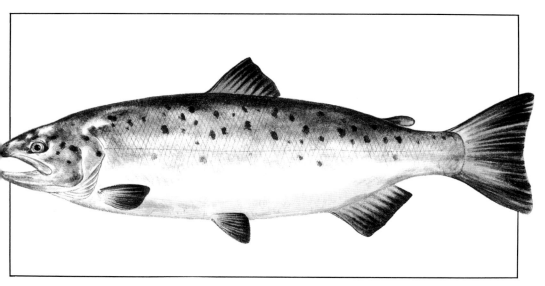

Classification: *Salmo salar*, family Salmonidae

Habitat: A migratory species which spends much of its life in salt water. Spawning fish are found in sea lochs, lakes and major rivers. Landlocked *Salmo salar* also exist

Range: In North American waters it occurs from Greenland to Cape Cod. In European waters from Russia to Portugal

Coloration: Sea run fish are blue/silver. Once into freshwater they change to dirty red in the case of the male and blackish silver in the female

Size: Up to a possible 30 kg (66 lb). Normally 3–4 kg (6.6–8.8 lb)

Description: Atlantic Salmon spawn in the autumn and early winter. Unlike the Chinook Salmon which spawns only once, the Atlantic Salmon may spawn on several occasions throughout its life. The newly-hatched salmon, or parr, remain in the river for 1–4 years. Initially trout-like in appearance, they change to a silver form known as smolt. At some time in those 4 years the salmon will head for the sea. Once they reach saltwater they may remain there for several years or return to spawn at the end of the first year. The latter fish are then known as grilse. During the course of that first year they grow from some 6 inches in length to a weight of 4–5 lb (2–2.5 kg). Three winters at sea may increase their weight to 15–30 lb (6.8–13.6 kg), while 4–6 years at sea results in fish that weigh 35–70 lb (18.8–37.6 kg). With rare exceptions Atlantic Salmon return to their parent river to spawn. The feeding grounds of the fish are off Greenland. Over-fishing has resulted in all-time low stocks.

Chinook Salmon

Classification: *Onchorhynchus tshawytscha*, family Salmonidae
Habitat: Large rivers of the Pacific Basin
Range: From Monterey, South California, north to Alaska
Coloration: Grey back, silver sides, the dorsal and caudal fins are speckled with black
Size: Up to 50 kg (110 lb)

Description: Because it is the largest of the salmon the chinook is often called the King Salmon. Chinook salmon spend the major part of their lives at sea. When they reach sexual maturity they migrate back to the river of their birth. These upstream migration runs may carry them as much as 1800 miles from the river mouth. Many perish running the hazards of rapids and waterfalls. Those that do survive change greatly in outward appearance. No longer sleek and silver, the fish are blackish with dark orange-red blotches. The tail becomes cherry red and the once finely-shaped jaws become grotesquely hooked and savage-looking. Once their eggs are shed the fish die. The young, or parr, remain in freshwater for one or two years. They then descend to the sea where they grow rapidly on a rich diet of anchovies, shrimps and prawns.

Chum Salmon

Classification: *Oncorhynchus keta*, family Salmonidae
Habitat: Parent river and open ocean
Range: From north California to Korea and Japan. Now also established in rivers leading into the Barents Sea.
Coloration: Dark greeny bronze or black shading to yellow green on the sides. Spawning fish turn very red on their sides with a pattern of light and dark vertical bars
Size: Normally 1.3–2.2 kg (3–5 lb)

Description: These fish normally spawn in the lower reaches of their chosen river system, the exception being Teslin Lake on the headwaters of the Yukon River. To reach this point the migrating salmon have to swim a gruelling 2000 miles, traversing rocky waters and boiling waterfalls. Chum salmon spawn in November/December. The eggs of these species are large, approaching 0.7 cm (0.3 in) in diameter. Migratory runs of chum salmon fluctuate widely from year to year. Some seasons the river may be bank to bank with spawning fish, the next only a few salmon may run up river. Chum salmon mature at 4 to 5 years. Within their range they are an important commercial catch, most of the meat being canned. In 1956 Russia introduced the Chum salmon to the Barents Sea area. Since this introduction the fish have become established in several Soviet rivers and also in northern Norway. Very much a predatory fish, the chum feeds on a constant diet of fish and crustaceans. It is said to be particularly fond of prawns, a pink dye in the prawn shells giving its flesh a distinctive pink tinge.

Coho Salmon

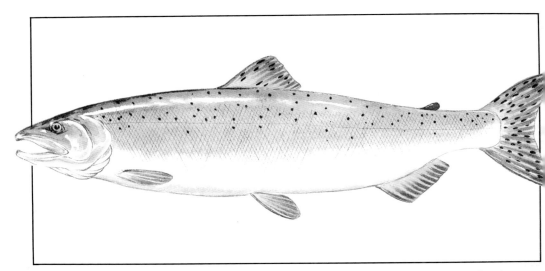

Classification: *Oncorhynchus kisutch*, family Salmonidae
Habitat: Open sea and parent river
Range: From California to Japan. It has also been introduced to the Great Lakes system where it has thrived
Coloration: Silvery overall with black spots
Size: 3–4 kg (6.6–8.8 lb)

Description: Sometimes called silver salmon, or hook nose salmon, the coho is a popular food fish. Spawning occurs between October and February, the eggs being shed in shallow redds dug in the gravel of ocean-linked rivers and streams. Once hatched most young coho stay for a year in their parent river, but occasionally some stay for three years before making their down-river run. Once saltwater is reached the coho remains within easy striking range of its own river system. They feed on anchovy, squid, herring and a surprisingly high proportion of crab larvae. One reason that it has flourished in American waters is that for the most part it spawns in small coastal rivers nor large enough to support hydroelectric schemes or irrigation complexes. Coho populations also range widely. Coho salmon originating in northern California range as far north as Washington; cohos from Washington extend as far north as the Queen Charlotte islands or south to north California. This constant interchange keeps the quality of fish stocks high.

Landlocked Salmon

Classification: *Salmo salar*, family Salmonidae

Habitat: Found in the Maine river drainage systems, landlocked salmon have been introduced into many places. Introduced into certain lakes in Argentina this fish has done extremely well

Range: Once limited the landlocked salmon range is constantly extended by strictly supervised restocking programs

Coloration: Similar to its sea run counterpart the landlocked salmon is silver with a heavy overlay of dark spots

Size: Between 1–4 kg (2.2–8.8 lb). Occasionally twice this weight

Description: Ichthyologists consider the landlocked salmon to be identical in all ways to the sea run Atlantic salmon. Like the Altantic salmon the landlocked once existed over a much greater natural range than it does today. Originally distributed in the Canadian maritime provinces, much of New England, Lake Ontario and a few lakes in New Yorks' Adirondacks, the landlocked was decimated by the encroachment of civilization. Deforestation on lake shores meant a gradual warming up of water temperatures. The landlocked salmon spawn between mid-October and the end of November. Migration takes place between the lakes and in-flowing rivers. The female fish dig a redd or nest in wind-rippled shallows where the bottom is comprised of clean gravel. Landlocked salmon fry feed on small aquatic insects and remain in the river of their birth for up to two years. Finally they migrate back into the lakes where they begin to feed on a variety of small food fish. Normally landlocked salmon reach a length of 76 cm (30 in) during the seventh year of their lives.

The Shads

Classification: Twaite shad (Europe – *Alosa fallax*; allis shad (Europe) – *Alosa alosa*; American shad – *Alosa sapidissima*; hickory shad – *Alosa mediocris*; skipjack herring – *Alosa chrysochloris*. Family Clupeidae

Habitat: The Atlantic and more recently the Pacific Ocean

Coloration: Silvery white, some species like the twaite and American shads have six dark spots from gill plate to dorsal fin. Others like the Allis shad have a single shoulder spot

Size: In European waters shad rarely attain a weight of more than 1 kg (2.2 lb). The American shad can reach weights in excess of 3 kg (6.6 lb)

Description: The Shads are a group of marine fish which migrate into rivers to spawn. In European waters the once prolific shad have been decimated by over-fishing and pollution. The River Severn is one of four British rivers to support a good run of spawning fish. In American waters the Alosa shad was originally found only in Atlantic waters, its range being from the Florida Keys north to the gulf of St. Lawrence. During the early 1870s these fish were introduced to the Californian coast. Since that restocking the shad have extended their range as far north as Alaska. Shad are plump, silver fish similar in shape to a herring. Strong swimmers with a large distinctive forked tail, they make excellent eating. The male fish mature at 3 to 4 years. Females may take up to 8 years to reach breeding age. Shad enter their spawning rivers in March or April. Once the spawn is shed the parent fish migrate back to the ocean. Shad eat shrimps, worms and small fish.

American Smelt

Description: Highly popular as a food fish the American smelt is a slender little fish with an adipose fin set behind its dorsal fin. This fin links it directly to the trout and the white fish. Smelt are a shoaling species which swarm in their millions during the April spawning run. Spawning normally occurs at night when the fish forsake deep water to ascend small streams and rivers. Landlocked smelt normally shoal at depths of 15–60 m (50–200 ft). They live on insects, zooplankton and tiny fish and shrimps. Smelt which live in saltwater make only a short inland spawning run, such a run lasting less than two weeks. A noted pan fish the American smelt run usually turns into a picnic carnival, fish being scooped up by the hundred for immediate cooking. Smelt provide many game fish with a constant supply of nutritious food. Salmon, trout, char and pike often rely on the smelt shoals for their everyday existence. On one or two of the larger lakes landlocked smelt are fished for by commercial fishing companies.

Classification: *Osmerus mordax*, family Osmeridae
Range: Along the east coast from Labrador through East Canada, south to New Jersey. Some north-eastern lakes hold landlocked smelt
Habitat: Normally a saltwater species which only enters freshwater to spawn
Coloration: Silvery coloured
Size: Maximum weight 170–226 gm (6–8 oz)

The Sturgeon Family

Classification: The white sturgeon – *Acipenser transmontanus*; lake sturgeon – *Acipenser fulvescens*; Atlantic sturgeon – *Acipenser oxyrhynchus*; shovelnose sturgeon – *Scaphirhynchus platorynchus*; pallid sturgeon – *Scaphirhynchus albus*. Family Acipenseridae

Habitat: Open sea, estuaries and large river systems depending on the species

Range: Pallid and shovelnose sturgeon are found in freshwater from the St. Laurence river to the Gulf of Mexico. The white sturgeon is found in Pacific coastal waters. The Atlantic sturgeon is a fish of the Eastern Seaboard

Coloration: A dull bronze brown

Size: The largest sturgeon is the Atlantic, which can reach a weight of 300 kg (661 lb) and a length of 3–4 m (9.8–13.0 ft)

Description: Sturgeon are basically a primitive, even prehistoric type of fish. The body skeleton is mostly cartilaginous. The skin is virtually scaleless but is protected by 5 to 7 rows of large bony shields. The head of all sturgeon ends in a snout. The mouth is fleshy and suckerlike situated well back from the snout on the underside of the head. Four sensory barbels hang in a row directly in front of the mouth. The single dorsal fin is sited close to the fish's tail. Extremely slow growing it takes many years for a sturgeon to reach maturity. All sturgeon are migratory but the freshwater species simply move up into feeder streams to shed eggs. Rather like an animated vacuum cleaner, sturgeon feed by slowly hoovering over the bottom silt, animal and vegetable matter being siphoned out and swallowed. Their normal diet includes insect larvae, shrimps, molluscs and small fish. Almost any small dead animal will be eaten. One giant sturgeon was found to contain the remains of a dead cat. Rated highly as a table fish, the sturgeon also yields eggs which sell as caviar. Left is a lake sturgeon.

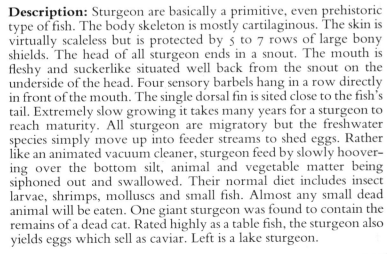

Tench

Classification: *Tinca tinca*, family Cyprinidae

Range: Britain, Europe and much of Asia. Tench have been introduced into S. Ireland where they have thrived

Habitat: Lakes, ponds, loughs, canals, reservoirs and slow flowing rivers

Coloration: Bronze green on the back and golden green on the sides. There is also a variety known as golden tench which is banana yellow, overlaid with a few black specks. Tench have tiny orange red eyes and a tiny barbule at each corner of the mouth.

Size: Maximum size is 3.5 kg (7.7 lb)

Description: The tench is a typical cyprinid which spends much of its life browsing through weed mud and silt. It has a thickset body with tiny flat body scales. These are covered by a thick layer of protective slime. Much prized as a food fish tench are extensively farmed in Europe and Asia. There is no market for these fish in England. Although their orange red eyes are tiny, tench appear to have good eyesight. Much of their food consists of midge larvae, pond snails, worms and freshwater mussels. Shellfish are taken whole, the shell being crushed by the powerful throat teeth. The shell remnants are then blown out through the mouth and gills. The pelvic fins of male tench are much larger and more rounded than those of the females. Spawning takes place in early summer, the eggs being shed in various weed beds or on projecting tree roots. Once shed the eggs and resulting fry are left to fend for themselves. In food-rich waters tench grow rapidly. In a less favoured environment the fish become stunted.

Brook Trout

Classification: *Salvelinus fontinalis*, family Salmonidae

Range: Originally a native of the north eastern part of the U.S.A., brook trout have been used to stock waters in Canada and Europe

Habitat: Lakes and cold water rivers and streams

Coloration: Dark olive back, green/silver sides and white underparts. The sides are dappled with creamy spots and tiny magenta spots. The lower fins are edged in white

Size: Up to a maximum to 4 kg (8.8 lb)

Description: Although very much akin to the trout family the brook trout is in fact related to the char. Extremely vulnerable to the pressures of civilization brook trout succumb quickly to dam building and waterbourne pollution. In the U.S.A. such problems led to the decimation of brook trout in many areas. In the wild state brook trout spawn in the autumn, the eggs being deposited in a nestlike depression sunk into the gravel. Both the eggs and the resulting fry are left to fend for themselves. Brook trout are greedy fish, worms, shrimps, aquatic insects and small fish being taken when available. Not normally a migratory species the brook trout of the north eastern coastal streams of America do go to sea. These sea run brook trout are called salters. Interestingly, it has a number of local names – brookie, speckled trout, eastern trout and square tail. During the past century brook trout have been extensively farmed by European fish farmers, most of the fish raised being used as stock fish.

Brown Trout

Classification: *Salmo trutta*, family Salmonidae

Habitat: Clear lakes, rivers, streams, lochs and reservoirs

Range: Originally a European species but not introduced on a world-wide basis

Coloration: Varies considerably from water to water. Normally golden brown on the back. Buttercup yellow on the sides. Underparts white. The body is covered with dark spots and rust or bright red dots

Size: Up to 10 kg (22 lb)

Description: The brown trout is an elongated fish. The tail is normally large and square cut and the wrist of the tail deep. The head is normally small and neat. Some fish, however, become total cannibals. When this occurs the jaws of the fish enlarge and change shape. The lower jaw forming a distinctive kype. Brown trout feed normally on nymphs and insect larvae, worms and winged insects. They are particularly fond of mayflies. Prior to a mayfly hatch hungry trout gorge on mayfly nymphs. Later when the spent may-flys begin to die on the water surface the trout rise to intercept each fly. Brown trout spawn during the winter months, the eggs being shed into crude nests or reeds excavated in clear gravel. Brown trout were introduced to the U.S.A. in 1883. Initially it was feared that the newly-introduced fish would destroy the native brook trout. Fortunately this did not happen. Today brown trout have been introduced to at least 42 states and to many parts of Canada and are thriving without damaging native trout stocks.

Cutthroat Trout

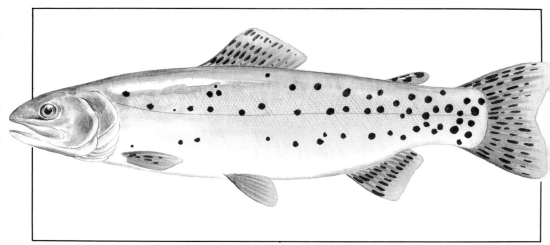

Classification: *Salmo clarki*, family Salmonidae
Habitat: Rivers and mountain lakes
Range: The western states of the U.S.A.
Coloration: Yellowish-green with red slashes below the head. The sides are marked by sparse but large spots
Size: Up to 18 kg (39.6 lb). More normally 2–3 kg (4.4–6.6 lb)

Description: Very much a fish of the western states the cutthroat is divided into many recognized subspecies e.g. piute cutthroat (*S. seleniris*); Yellowstone cutthroat (*S. lewis*); Utah cutthroat (*S. utah*); Colorado cutthroat (*S. pleubiticus*) and the Rio Grande (*S. virginalis*) to mention just a few. In the wild state cutthroat also hybridize with rainbow trout. Cutthroats normally spawn in late winter and early spring, the eggs being shed in shallow depressions on redds. Normally cutthroat spawn for the first time in their fourth year. After this, spawning occurs every other year. Where these fish live in rivers which flow into the sea, a sea run version can be found, such fish normally staying within easy range of their parent river. Sea run fish spawn annually. Cutthroat feed on insects, shrimps, and a variety of small fish. The largest subspecies, the Lahontan cutthroat (*Salmo henshani*) is found in the Lahontan drainage systems of Nevada and California. This particular fish is unique in its tolerance of alkaline water. The smallest subspecies (max. length 30 cm (12 in)) is native only to the headwaters of Silver King Creek in California and is totally protected.

Golden Trout

Classification: *Salmo agua Bonita*, family Salmonidae

Habitat: Streams and clear lakes

Range: Once only found in the headwaters of the Kern River in California, this fish has been introduced to waters in Wyoming, Washington and Idaho

Coloration: Probably the most beautiful of all trout, the golden has a cadium-yellow belly, yellow sides, a broad carmine body stripe overlaid with 10 dark blotches. It has orange tipped dorsal fin and white tipped pelvic and anal fin. The dorsal and tail fin are heavily spotted

Size: From 0.5–3 kg. (6.6 lb)

Description: Throughout most of its range the golden trout survives on a comparatively limited food supply. In the lakes of the Sierra Nevada mountain regions these fish feed mainly on caddisfly larvae and midge larvae. They also eat crustaceans when available. In more food rich waters, small fish are also taken. There is also a Mexican golden trout (*Salmo chrystogaster*) first described as late as 1959. Its total range is 56×72 km (35×45 miles), the fish being confined to the Fuente, Sinola and Culiacan river systems in southwest Chihuahua and north-western Durango. A striking feature of this Mexican trout is the bright orange colour below the jaw and on the lower belly. Little is known of the breeding habits of either the golden or the Mexican golden trout. Both fish are thought to spawn in the early spring. In streams the eggs are shed in well-oxygenated shallows. Lake fish also seek marginal shallows in which to deposit their eggs. Once laid the eggs are left to develop by themselves. The young trout feed mainly on zooplankton and tiny aquatic larvae.

Lake Trout

Classification: *Salvelinus namaycus*, family Salmonidae

Habitat: A fish of the northern Great Lakes with a preference for extremely deep water

Range: Throughout the northern portion of north America

Coloration: Dark grey with an overlay of small pale spots

Size: Up to 25 kg (55 lb)

Description: The lake trout is the largest fish in the trout group and is a symbol of the Great Lakes. In the salmon family it is exceeded only by the giant chinook salmon. Once an important commercial species, the lake trout population declined drastically during a massive lamprey invasion. There are signs, however, that lake trout are staging a comeback. Lake trout have many local names. In Alaska they are known as mackinaw trout, in Maine as togue. Lake trout will eat insects, but by inclination they are natural predators. Small fish such as smelt, white fish and minnow, such as ciscoe, making up the bulk of their food intake. Found at depths of more than 30 m (100 ft) lake trout are very much a cold water species. Spawning occurs during the autumn months when the fish move into the marginal shallows to shed their eggs. Spawning is a haphazard affair, the eggs being dropped at random amongst rocks and patches of marginal gravel. Once spawning is complete the parent fish move back to the deeps.

Rainbow Trout

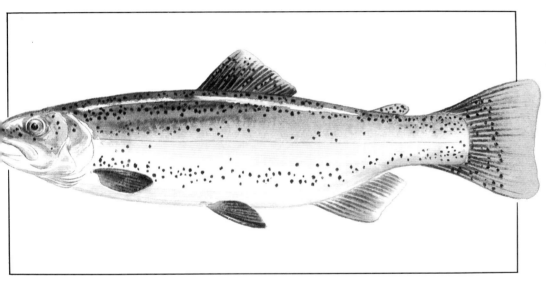

Classification: *Salmo gardnairi*, family Salmonidae

Habitat: Lakes, rivers and streams. There is also a sea run rainbow called a steelhead

Range: Originally a native of the western slope of the Pacific from Alaska to Mexico, this species has been widely stocked throughout the world

Coloration: Due to intensive selective breeding, rainbow trout can be found in many colour forms. The natural colour is blue brown on the back, iridescent magenta on the sides and silvery white on the belly

Size: Up to 16 kg (35.2 lb) in the wild state

Description: The name rainbow trout derives from the broad magenta side band that extends along the lateral line from head to tail. Very much a cold water species, rainbows are a hardier breed than brown trout. Though an American species, rainbow have become naturalized in many parts of the world. Introduced into Britain during the 1880s rainbows have become the standard stock fish. In American waters rainbows spawn at any time from February to June. This breeding period is different in other parts of the world. Spawning rainbows dig large pits in the shallow gravely sections of their home water. Spawning river rainbows migrate upstream. Lake fish seek out inflowing streams in which to breed. Once the eggs are deposited in the gravel they are left to hatch on their own. Sea run rainbows, called steelheads, are simply river fish that decide to spend much of their life in salt water. Rugged and spectacular fish, they can jump ten foot waterfalls in the urge to reach their upstream spawning grounds.

Walleye, Zander, and Sauger

Classification: Walleye – *Stizostedion lucioperca*; Zander – *S. vitreum vitreum*; Sauger – *S. canadense*. Family Percidae
Habitat: Rivers, lakes, reservoirs and the Great Lakes of North America
Range: North America for walleye and sauger. Zander in Northern Europe and the eastern half of England
Coloration: Walleye, zander, sauger, olive/bronze back, blotched, brassy-yellow sides, white underparts. The walleye has a dark spot at the rear of the dorsal fins. Walleye as its name implies has opaque-looking eyes
Size: Maximum for walleye/zander is around 6–8 kg (13.2–17.6 lb). Sauger are much smaller

Description: Highly predatory these fish have no established territory, instead following their prey fish from one feeding ground to the next. Very much solitary feeders these fish normally only gather at spawning times. Spawning takes place in shallow water where the eggs are shed on sand, gravel or rocks. The young fish are left to fend for themselves. Many are in fact eaten by their own parents. Nature compensates for this by allowing the young fish to grow rapidly. Most reach a length of 30.4–35.5 cm (12–14 in) by the end of the third year. In Britain, zander were introduced during the last century to lakes in the grounds of Woburn Abbey. Since that period legal and illegal stockings has led to a more widespread distribution. In the U.S.A. the walleye is a popular table fish. To satisfy the market, commerical fisheries operate in many areas where walleye are common. The walleye is known by over sixty colloquial names such as yellow pike, pike perch, jack salmon, blind pike and dore. Left is a walleye.